Norman Vincent Peale

How to cope with ten of life's toughest problems

GUIDEPOSTS ASSOCIATES, INC., CARMEL, NEW YORK 10512

CONTENTS

FOREWORD

A few months ago the editors of Guideposts magazine asked me to put together ten articles dealing with some tough everyday problems common to us all. The subjects I chose are typical of the human situations we try to deal with in Guideposts, an interfaith magazine read by approximately six million people each month.

Over the years I have had people come to me asking help with just about every problem imaginable, which is not surprising. As a minister I have been available and concerned, and when trouble comes people often turn to their ministers first. When you have a problem too big to handle, consider discussing it with your minister. Chances are good he will be able to help or he will be able to direct you to someone who can.

But I always have believed that there is much we can do for ourselves. God in His infinite wisdom gave us resources to deal with life's thorny problems. Some of the suggestions in this book are just good common sense; others are a little more involved but they have been tested in the school of experience, and I can attest to the fact that the methods work. These ten problems represent some of the most frequent difficulties people bring to me. They range from financial concerns and marriage troubles to poor health, grief and discouragement. I hope and pray that you find this book helpful. Read it, keep it for future reference, put its ideas to use and share them with others.

God bless you.

Norman Vincent Peale

1. HOW TO COPE WITH FEAR

"What can I do about my fears?" is a plea I hear often.

The trouble is not fears in the plural, but fear itself. For fear is a mental attitude that can pervade all of life.

At my farm in Pawling, New York, we had to take down a big old tree recently. When the tree men came around, I thought they would start at once at the base of the trunk. But that wasn't the way they did it at all.

They cut the tree down in three stages. First, they climbed up into the tree and started sawing off the branches. Finally, only the big tall shaft of the trunk remained. For the second operation they got out a power saw and cut the trunk off close to the ground.

The third step was to bulldoze into the earth and pull out the roots. After they leveled off the ground, we planted grass seed. Presently you would never know that the tree had been there.

It occurred to me that you can go at your fears the same way. Snip off the little ones first.

1

How do you do this? Well, when you go around locking the doors in your house each night, stop trying each knob two or three extra times to be sure it is locked. If you read in the paper that there is a flu epidemic in your town, don't say, "I suppose I will be getting it next." Stop saying fear statements and soon you will tend toward stopping fear thoughts. So much for the little branches.

Now let's bring up the big power saw because we are now about to take down the main trunk of our fear. Let's give a name to the power saw. Love. How can you cut fear off by love? Do you remember that verse in the Bible: *Perfect love casteth out fear?* Well, I have always felt that love was a very sharp instrument. It is a whirling buzz saw that can go sharply through fear and cut it aside.

This verse means that we are to love God, love Him completely.

But you may say, "How do you love God? He is so vague. I can love my wife, my children. But how can I love God? I can love a person but how can I love a vast idea?"

Wait a minute! God is a person. He is Jesus Christ, the person you read about in the New Testament. Every night before you go to bed read one or two chapters from the Gospels. When you have read Matthew, Mark, Luke and John, read them again, and reread them and read them again until you actually know Jesus Christ, personally know Him.

As you get acquainted with Him you will love Him. And as you love Him you will trust Him. As you trust, you will give yourself to Him and as you give yourself you will give Him your fears. This is how perfect love casteth out fear.

As you continue this practice the big, major trunk of your fear will no longer exist. It only remains now to go below the surface and get the roots that gave rise to the whole bad business of fear.

So the final stage is to take that bulldozer, which we will

name faith, and grub out the old roots on which the tree of fear in your life grew.

What are the roots of fear? We pick up much of our fear in childhood.

Normal fear, which means the element of caution, is sensible. Without it a person would be a fool. But the trouble is that normal fear so easily becomes abnormal fear. And so often a network of fear roots is formed out of our childish fears of the unknown, of the dark, and of the fears of other people around us.

Other roots of fear are formed by sin. Every time you sin, you become afraid that you will be found out, that you are going to be punished. You develop guilty feelings. Your mind becomes mixed up in its values because it rationalizes, trying to make black into white, telling you that what you did really is not wrong. So, your life becomes a mess of lies, equivocations. The result is that obsessions and psychoses develop. And out of it is created vague, sinister fear which can ultimately insinuate itself into every area of your life.

To get this messy stuff out, bring up the bulldozer and get down into your mind with its sharp, clean blade of faith and root out the fear. Say to yourself, "I believe that Jesus Christ can forgive my sin. I ask Him to do so now. I have faith that my life is redeemed."

The combination of love and faith can overcome any fear. This is the great good news that Jesus has for us.

2. HOW TO COPE WITH FATIGUE

Fatigue—what a common complaint it is! Physicians hear about it constantly. "I'm so tired, doctor; I just don't seem to have the energy to get through the day!" Ministers see it too, etched on the faces of people who come to them for help with spiritual or emotional problems.

Think of the problems caused by fatigue: industrial accidents, deaths on the highway, even aviation fatalities. Fatigue vastly increases personal problems of all kinds, too. Just the other day a divorced woman came to me for counseling, lonely, tense, nervous. "What caused your divorce?" I asked her. "I think," she said slowly, "it was because both of us were tired all the time. And when we were tired, it was so easy to quarrel." Of course it was! Fatigue impairs judgment and weakens self-control.

Doctors tell us that there are three kinds of fatigue. The first is pathological, a sign of actual disease. Anyone who is extremely tired all the time should see a physician.

4

The second kind is physiological fatigue—chemical reactions in the blood that leave healthy people temporarily tired. There is nothing wrong with physiological tiredness if normal recovery occurs within a reasonable time. Hard work or hard exercise *should* leave you feeling healthily tired.

The third kind of fatigue is psychological. It can be produced by prolonged internal conflict, by anxiety, by many forms of emotional maladjustment. Some doctors claim that when a person complains of chronic exhaustion, chances run as high as 80 percent that he is suffering from some form of psychological fatigue.

Suppose you have a fatigue problem and suppose it belongs in this category—what can you do? How can you prevent psychological fatigue, or at least minimize it? How can you turn yourself from a low-energy person, or a no-energy person, into a high-energy person? Let me offer a few suggestions.

To begin with, take a good, long, honest look at yourself. Is your life an open book, or are there dark places in it? "The soul that sinneth," says the Bible, "it shall die." This is one way of saying that the guilt you feel from any wrongdoing is a poison that brings fatigue and paralysis to the mind—and ultimately to the body. Asking the Lord for forgiveness and doing what you can to make amends for the sin will remove this kind of poison from your body.

Are you harboring resentment or grudges against anyone? Sustained anger is a staggering load to carry around, a deadly waste of energy. If you have such feuds or animosities in your life, why not do what the Bible says: "Go and be reconciled to your brother." Until you do, your sources of energy are going to be impaired or blocked.

Are you a chronic worrier? Nothing is more exhausting than prolonged anxiety. Why not let faith help here, too? "Take no thought for the morrow," Jesus said. The problems of today, He added, were enough to keep anyone busy. So why not just hand over future perplexities and fears to Him? He will carry the burden for you, if you will just let Him.

Ask yourself if to some extent your fatigue may be imaginary. Are you telling yourself that you are "too tired" to tackle this job or attempt that task because you know it may be difficult, or because you are afraid of failure? Are you "too tired" to make that trip because you don't really want to see the person you're suppose to visit? This kind of "motivational" fatigue is a lot more common than most people realize.

Make a little study of your energy patterns. All of us have more get up-and-go at certain times than at others. Why not plan to tackle your most difficult or stressful problems when your energy is at its peak?

Try to eliminate from your life things that upset or frustrate you. In my own case, for example, I have found that clutter is a great fatigue-producer. I simply cannot think clearly or work effectively in a messy room or on a cluttered desk. My wife is well aware of this quirk of mine and tries to keep our home as neat as a pin. So if your nerves are jangled by untidiness or intrusive noises or garish colors—anything within your power to control—eliminate these things. Your energy-quotient will go up.

Give yourself something pleasant to look forward to. Anticipation is a great tonic. In a study made of industrial workers, it was found that at the end of a hard day's work some employees were completely fatigued, while others had plenty of energy left. The difference, the survey proved, was that the tired workers had nothing to look forward to after quitting time—no diversions, no plans—whereas the energetic ones had.

As often as possible, do something at which you excel. The exercise of any skill or talent always raises the spirits, increases confidence, heightens enthusiasm. Actually, it has been shown in laboratory tests that a skilled or talented worker burns up less energy than an unskilled one. That is why so many persons of genius seem to be virtually tireless; their skill and confidence enable them to soar above the barriers that impede others.

Finally—and this may be the most important suggestion of all—think of yourself not as a *source* of energy but as a *channel* for energy. The life force that animates us all does not come from any human source. It comes from God. It stands to reason, therefore, that if we keep as close to God as we can and keep the channels open, His power will flow through us, minimizing fatigue and turning us into high-energy people.

Christ is the contact point—that is the heart of the message of Christianity. "I am come that they might have life," Jesus said, "and have it more abundantly."

Life—energy—these terms are almost synonymous. For a Christian there is no greater hope, no greater promise.

3. HOW TO COPE WITH A TROUBLED MARRIAGE

Not long ago, I received a letter from a couple I had married. On the verge of divorce, they asked my advice. This is what I told them:

Dear Kenneth:

I have your letter in which you say that you and Nancy are no longer happy together, that you find it increasingly difficult to communicate, and that you are wondering whether it might not be best for all concerned to end your marriage. You add that, since I was the minister who married you, both of you feel you owe it to me to talk the situation over before doing anything final. And you end by saying that you hope I will understand.

Well, I do understand, I understand that two people who stood before me nine years ago and promised to love and cherish each other forever are about to join the ranks of the more than 800,000 Americans who every year decide to demonstrate publicly that they lack the courage, intelligence and unselfishness to make a marriage work.

I shall be glad to see you here in my office one week from today—under certain conditions. If you accept them—there may be some point in our meeting. Otherwise I see little reason to waste my time—or yours.

Let me talk for a moment in generalities before I come to the specifics. You say that you and Nancy are no longer happy together. Do you really believe that constant happiness is guaranteed in marriage or in any other aspect of life? Aren't you mature enough to know that every marriage has its areas of friction, and that the stresses change as you move through the years? You will never solve all your problems. You would be bored if you did.

This belief that each of you is entitled to *receive* happiness is at the bottom of your trouble. You are not entitled to any such thing! The marriage ceremony doesn't even mention the word. What you do have is the privilege and the problem of *giving* happiness. When you master that art, you discover that you can't give it without getting it back. But apparently neither of you has mastered the art.

I sometimes wonder if this obsession with having things just the way we want them—and sulking if they're not—isn't becoming a kind of American disease. Somehow we must get a quality of toughness and endurance back into our concept of marriage. We have got to stop thinking of it as a "maybe" proposition—maybe it will work, maybe it won't—and if it doesn't we can always shuffle the cards and deal again.

Certainly there are some cases where a marriage has been allowed to die and nothing can revive it. I don't think you two have reached that point. But you *will* reach it unless you take some constructive action, and take it quickly.

You say you would like to talk with me. All right. I shall be glad to meet you one week from today—if, between now and then, you and Nancy will agree to an experiment.

9

Each day for six days I want you to set aside one half-hour in which you follow exactly the instructions I am about to give you.

I don't guarantee that they will be pleasant half hours or easy ones. At first, indeed, you may feel that you are getting nowhere. But at least the equipment is simple. You will need an alarm clock—preferably an old one with a loud tick—two chairs, a quiet room where you will not be disturbed, and a determination to carry through with the experiment once you have started it.

There is one other requirement: for this one week I want you both to stop drinking. Perhaps neither of you drinks much, perhaps you are convinced that alcohol is not a significant factor in your difficulties. But even in small amounts—especially when relations between people are strained—alcohol lowers the threshold of irritability.

The technique of the daily half hour is simple. Go into the room together, close the door, set the alarm clock to ring in 30 minutes, and place it where both of you can watch it. Now mentally divide the half-hour into six five-minute periods. There are six steps in the technique.

In the first *five minutes* project yourselves into the future. This can be done separately and silently by each of you, but it must be done with intensity and realism. You must try to visualize things as they will be if your marriage breaks up.

Kenneth, ask yourself coldly and logically what happens to a man when he gets a divorce. He loses his home; the comfort, the familiarity, the companionship, the knowledge that his laundry will be sent out, that his meals will appear. He usually loses his children—possibly their respect and affection, certainly most of their companionship and physical presence. Alimony or support requirements may cripple his earning power for years. He will certainly lose some friends: in these marital break-ups, people tend to side with the wife. He may find that in his business or profession he has gained the enmity of people who can influence his career.

Nancy, in my many years as a minister I have learned that the woman is the one who suffers most, emotionally, from a divorce. Her sense of failure as a person is greater than the man's; her loneliness is a more complete loneliness. A man has his work to fall back on, with its demands and disciplines and contacts. A woman often does not. It is much more difficult for her to find a sexual substitute for marriage. If she has children, her chances of remarrying are far less than the man's.

In the *second five minutes*, I want each of you to make a supreme effort to stop judging each other, and examine yourselves. This is never easy to do. But the blame in these matters is never onesided. Ask yourself, with all the honesty you can command, certain uncomfortable questions. Have you magnified this or that grievance out of all proportion? Have you been too rigid in your demands? Have you refused to compromise on key issues? (Compromise doesn't mean giving in, you know.) Have you judged your marriage partner guilty of all these things while leaving yourself exempt? Doesn't the law of averages whisper that at least *sometimes* you must be in the wrong?

If you really think on these things, you will find that the silence surrounding both of you will seem very loud. Do you know why I recommended an alarm clock with a loud tick? Because one man who tried this experiment told me that at the end of five minutes it seemed to him that the clock was repeating over and over again the word that was at the bottom of all his trouble: *self, self, self, self . . .*

The *third five minutes* I want you to spend silently thinking about your children. You say in your letter that you feel an atmosphere of discord and hostility in the home may well be worse for them than the dislocations of

11

a divorce. But this selfish rationalization is based on an assumption that is not necessarily true, the assumption that the hostility and discord are inevitable and will go on forever.

Certainly quarreling parents are bad for children, especially if they lack the self-control to do their fighting in private. But an uneasy home with two parents may well be better than a broken home with one. It has been my observation that when children become greatly upset in these situations, the thing that bothers them most is the fear that their parents are going to split up, and that they are going to lose one or the other.

Nancy, where the welfare of the children is concerned, I think you are the one who must refuse to be stampeded into an unwise course of action. I have never forgotten a girl I knew whose husband came home from overseas at the end of World War II and told her that he had fallen in love with an American Army nurse in France and wanted a divorce so that he could marry her. The wife quietly but firmly refused to let him go. She said that their children needed a father, that theirs had been a good marriage once and it could be a good marriage again. She put aside her own hurt feelings and wounded pride. She simply waited, month after month. Finally the other woman got bored and discouraged and married someone else. The husband came back, hesitantly and perhaps a bit resentfully. But the children did need him, he did love them, and in the end the marriage was rebuilt and has lasted solidly ever since.

Now let's assume that you are at the mid-point of this half-hour experiment. For 15 minutes you have been sitting in silence. Now it is time for you to begin to communicate with each other, and in this *fourth five minute period* I want each of you, taking turns on alternate days, to read aloud four verses from the Bible: the thirteenth chapter of St. Paul's first epistle to the Corinthians,

12

verses four through seven. Fewer than 60 words, but they contain the most profound and inclusive definition of love ever written.

The words will sound familiar because you have heard them often. But I doubt that you have ever taken time to meditate on just what St. Paul meant when he said that love suffers long and is kind, that love is not easily provoked, that love endures all things (not *some* things, all things!) Read those four verses aloud, close the Book, and think about them for five minutes.

The *fifth step* in the experiment is the old nostalgic game called, "Do you remember?" During this five minutes each of you must recall from the past and bring to the other's attention some episode, however minor, that you remember because it was a moment of harmony and closeness. Perhaps the time you walked together on some beach at sunrise, hand in hand, looking for shells. Perhaps the time you sat up all night with a sick child. Perhaps some tender and ludicrous moment that turned into a family joke. Again, there need be no analysis, no discussion. Just recognition of the fact that once there was love and sharing.

Finally, at the beginning of the *last five-minute period*, I want each of you to hold one other Biblical phrase in your mind: *Be still—and know that I am God*. I don't know what your concept of God may be, whether you think of Him as a loving Father or some vast impersonal Force behind an inhuman, mechanistic universe. But in any case, speaking aloud, I want each of you to tell that Concept just what you think has gone wrong with your marriage, and what part you feel you played in it. Speak from the bottom of your soul and heart.

This, of course, is a form of prayer, and you may hesitate or even balk at this final requirement. But I can tell you this: I have married hundreds of couples and counseled with hundreds of others, and I have never yet known a marriage where the partners had—or acquired—the habit of praying aloud together that ended in the divorce court.

It need not be a lengthy process; perhaps one minute will do. And there is no set formula. But I will guarantee you this: if you try you will find yourself speaking in a different tone of voice and, by the time that alarm clock rings, your whole point of view will be subtly changed.

Not long ago a colleague of mine preached a sermon in which he said that he had found in one short sentence the answer to many of life's thorniest problems. That sentence was: "The way out is the way through." He meant that when you're faced with a difficult situation, you can't solve it by running away, or trying to squirm around or under it, or pretending it isn't there. You have to plough straight through it, live straight through it, until you come out on the other side.

This takes courage, certainly, and it takes facing of facts. It takes persistence, determination, control, all the qualities of mind and heart that add up to "stickability," which I sometimes think is the most valuable human quality of all. But that's what you and Nancy need, Kenneth. You think your marriage is unhappy, and so you talk of ending it. But that's not the way out. The way out is the way through, and I am certain that if you and Nancy will take courage in both hands and hang on long enough, you will achieve a closeness that will make your honeymoon years seem like puppy love.

Something in you, some wisdom deeper than your conscious mind knows this: otherwise you never would have written to me. Come and see me a week from now. The way out is the way through, and there is a way through. With God's help I think, I hope, I *know* that we can find it.

Affectionately,
Norman

14

4. HOW TO COPE WITH CRITICISM

Only two things in life are certain, Benjamin Franklin once remarked: death and taxes. But there is one other unpleasant certainty: criticism. No one escapes it entirely. And often our careers, our emotional stability, our happiness depend on how we react to it.

There are really two kinds of criticism: the gentle, tactful, constructive variety (which no one gets much of!); and the blunt, harsh, hostile kind. I can speak with wry authority about this second kind. For years, everything in my life went fairly well. Then some very vocal critics of my writings and my ministry appeared. When the storm arose, I didn't know how to handle it. I had to learn—the hard way!

What I learned mainly is that if you're a sensitive person, or an honest one, you can't just brush criticism aside or pretend it's not there. You have to face up to it on three levels; the emotional, the rational and the practical.

15

Controlling your emotional reaction is the hardest. Criticism is a direct attack on your self-esteem. So it is all too easy to react with resentment and anger. But this just makes you more vulnerable; if all you do is resent your critic, you are only poisoning yourself.

The first step, then, is to *force* yourself to be dispassionate. This never is easy, but it can be done. I once went to see Herbert Hoover, surely one of the most unjustly maligned men of our era. "Mr. President," I said to him, "how did you keep from being embittered by all that criticism during your Presidency?"

"Well," said Mr. Hoover with a smile, "I can think of two possible answers. In the first place, as you know, I'm an engineer, trained to anticipate problems. I knew that sooner or later every one of my predecessors had had to face a barrage of criticism. So, when I moved into the White House, I was prepared. That was one thing.

"The other," he said gently, "is that I'm a Quaker." I knew what he meant: Quakers believe in an inner quietness, a peace that will come if you empty your heart of resentment and bitterness. When a man has this God-given inner calm, he is not likely to be disturbed by man-made storms.

The Bible, with its profound insight into human nature, says, *pray* for your critics; bless them that hurt you. This may seem preposterous to someone smarting under the lash of undeserved criticism, but the amazing truth is that it does relieve the hurt. It's effective, because the human mind can hold only one idea at a time. If you force yourself to pray for your critic, you cannot simultaneously brood about the injury that has been done to you.

Yet another way to steady your emotions when you find yourself under attack is to reflect that strong men and women always have been criticized. If your life has any vitality at all, if you are determined to get things done, you are going to encounter hostility and opposition. The

16

greatest Man who ever walked this earth was bitterly criticized, condemned and finally crucified by contemporaries who could not stand the impact of His revolutionary ideas.

Abraham Lincoln, today probably our most beloved President, said, "If I were to try to read, much less answer, all the attacks made on me, this shop might as well be closed for any other business. I do the very best I know how, the very best I can. If the end brings me out all right, what is said against me won't amount to anything. If the end brings me out wrong, ten angels swearing I was right would make no difference."

The second step in coping with criticism is to be rational. Take up the criticism and examine it objectively, for as Leschetizky, the great piano teacher, used to say, "We learn much from the disagreeable things people say, for they make us *think*; whereas the good things only make us glad."

Ask yourself honestly if there is any truth in the criticism. Beware of self-excuses or rationalizations; if you give in to these, you may just compound the original error. If you are forced to the conclusion that what your critic is saying is true, the best thing to do is admit it. This in itself will silence him. After all, if you agree with him, what more can he say? Besides, it's astonishing how people rally to the side of someone who can admit he's wrong.

Another rational approach is to examine the qualifications of your critic. Has he reason to be spiteful or jealous? Then perhaps you can dismiss his words. Is he reputable and sincere? If so, you had better weigh his remarks.

I remember well an episode of a few years ago. The dean of a famous divinity school had made a speech in which he said some very harsh things about me. When reporters swooped down on me, clamoring for a reply, I didn't even know what the dean had said. One of the reporters was more than happy to tell me. I was upset, but

17

I took a deep breath and said that my critic was an eminent man whose judgment I respected. I added that therefore I had better re-examine my message and my methods, and that if I found any error, I would try to correct it.

I'll never forget the expressions on those reporters' faces. They were looking for a battle—and they were unable to stir one up.

Is there anything on the *practical* level that you can do in dealing with criticism? Yes, you can try to help your critic. For criticism is a two-edged sword, and often it is the poisoned edge that cuts the person who wields it.

Gossip, for example, is nothing but criticism motivated by jealously or insecurity. Small people often find it easier to tear someone else down than to try to build themselves up. But what is their reward? No one trusts them. In the end, no one believes them.

The Bible commands us to return good for evil. This is not pious nonsense; kindness *is* stronger than malice. I remember my father telling about a reporter he knew who covered William McKinley's campaign for the Presidency. His newspaper was violently opposed to McKinley, and he was supposed to travel on the train with the candidate and send back negative stories at every opportunity.

At first he did—and McKinley knew it. But one bitterly cold afternoon the reporter fell asleep huddled on the green plush seat of the unheated car. McKinley came by, stopped and spread his overcoat over the man. When the reporter awoke and found out what had happened, he resigned from his job. He couldn't go on maligning a man big enough to answer his criticisms by befriending him.

Constant critics are often warped and unhappy people, clutching at false importance, trying to cover up their own inadequacies by pointing out the failings of other people. The Christian thing to do when you encounter hostility in another person is to try to get behind the anger, to understand what causes it, and to remove the cause for the other person's sake as well as for your own.

As Disraeli once remarked, "It is much easier to be critical than correct," so there will always be plenty of critics in the world. You can defend yourself against the unkind ones by learning to control your emotional reactions, by adopting a calm and rational attitude and by honestly trying to help your critics rid themselves of their anger. But, in the last analysis, your best defense is your own day-to-day conduct. It is keeping your moral standards high. It is having a clear conscience. It is living a life without any necessity whatever for deception or lies or concealment.

If you will obey the Ten Commandments, if you will do your best to live up to the Golden Rule, the slings and arrows of self-appointed critics will make little impression on you because—as the Bible puts it—you will be wearing the armor of righteousness. And the Bible—as usual—is right.

5. HOW TO COPE WITH
POOR HEALTH

There is a wonderful passage in Isaiah which describes how anybody can be healthy, vital and alive. How glorious it is—Isaiah 40:31—"But they that wait upon the Lord shall renew their strength; they shall mount up with wings as eagles; they shall run, and not be weary; and they shall walk, and not faint."

Did you ever see an eagle rise up? I took off on a 747 the other day, but it couldn't compare with the way an eagle rises up or takes off. I saw one leave a rocky crag in the Yosemite National Park one time. He reached for the sky, of which he was the master. "They that wait upon the Lord . . . shall mount up with wings as eagles,". but that isn't the end: "they shall run, and not be weary." They won't get tired. Even that isn't the end: ". . . and they shall walk, and not faint."

Almighty God built energy into us when we were born. He implanted in us the life force, and true faith can keep this life force alive. A friend of mine consulted a Park Avenue physician one day, a very famous doctor in New York. After careful examination and meticulous study of the reports of tests, the doctor said to the patient, "All of my scientific findings point to serious trouble ahead for you. In fact, I must tell you that your life expectancy is very limited."

The patient was visibly stunned and asked, "How long, doctor?"

"Well," replied the doctor, "I won't give you a specific time, but it's limited."

The man asked further, "Is there no hope for me?"

Now this was a wonderful doctor. "Yes," he said, "there is hope for you if you will have hope. Remember, my friend, I am only a human person who works with God. We treat the patient; God heals him. If you will somehow find your way back to a deep relationship with God, you may prove my prognosis to be in error."

The man left the doctor's office with no destination in mind or sense of guidance. He just started walking up Park Avenue. It was a beautiful spring day and he began to notice the trees and the flower beds along the avenue. In the warm April sunshine the flowers were beginning to push through the good earth. Buds that would soon be leaves were beginning to come out on the trees. The thought occurred to him, "Isn't this strange; these trees and these perennial flowers seem to know that it is spring and they are emerging to new life. Here is the ineffable miracle of nature. Aren't the operations in the natural world also applicable to the physical world? Couldn't the same miracle work in me?"

So, standing there on that great avenue, he did a curious thing, a very curious thing; and I have done the same thing many times since he told me about it. Drawing himself up, he said, "I now affirm the emergence in me of the life force. What is happening in nature is now happening in my physical body." He maintained this affirmation and repeated it over and over again for days.

He continued his visits to the doctor. Once in a while the doctor nodded his head with a smile. He seemed pleased, but said very little. Finally, after many months, the physician said to his patient, "The conditions that plagued you some months ago no longer exist. You are a healthy, vital man." And when the man told the doctor what he had done, this very great physician, with a joyous look on his face, said, "You have thought and prayed and affirmed your way back to health." What a wonderful lesson this should be to us all.

What are some of the many things a person needs to do if he wants to be healthy, vital and alive? Number one, of course, is to wash out of the mind all the old, tired, dead, listless, unhappy, unworthy thoughts that clutter the mind. Dr. Sara Jordan of the Lahey Clinic in Boston suggests that you give your mind a shampoo every day. If this is done, there will be fewer people in our clinics. A basic cause of much illness is a lesion in the soul, which is caused by sickness in the mind. Hate, resentment, dishonesty, inferiority and other debilitating thoughts draw and siphon off healthiness.

One day in New York City I was riding in a taxicab with three other men. It was a beautiful day, and I had a joyous feeling about it. As we got into the taxicab I said to the driver, "Isn't this a terrific day!"

He replied. "So what? Maybe it's all right now, but it'll rain before night, maybe snow," and various other negativisms. As we rode along these other men were calling me "doctor" all the while. Finally the driver turned around, thinking he had a physician in the cab and might get a little free treatment, and he said, "Say, doc, you know, I have pains in my back all the time."

"Why," I said, "you shouldn't have pains in your back. How old are you?"

"I'm 37," he replied, "I just ache all over. Furthermore, I can't eat very well because I have pains in my stomach, and I don't feel good. What do you think may be wrong with me?"

"Look, my friend," I said, "it's not possible to practice medicine in taxicabs, but you seem to be a nice fellow, and I think I can diagnose your problem. What I really think you have is psychosclerosis." Well, this shocked him so that he nearly ran up on the sidewalk.

"Psychosclerosis?" He said. "What in the world is that?"

Now, I wasn't too sure myself, but I said, "You know about arteriosclerosis, don't you?"

"No," he said, "I don't know what that is."

"Well, that means hardening of the arteries, and that's a bad thing to get. But psychosclerosis is infinitely worse. That means hardening of the thoughts. Ever since I've been in this taxicab you've been exhibiting the symptoms of psychosclerosis. And if you don't get over the psychosclerosis, the next thing you know you'll have arteriosclerosis."

This really got to him and he said, "What in the world am I going to do about it?"

"I'll tell you. Come to my office and we'll give you a treatment." And I handed him my card.

'Why, you're not a doctor of medicine; you're a religious doctor."

"Yes," I said, "but that is the kind of doctor you need. You don't need a medical doctor nearly as much as you need a doctor of the mind and a doctor of the soul." Well, he made an appearance at the church; we gave him a spiritual treatment; and after a while he was cured of his "psychosclerosis." And what it cost him was a complete giving of himself in surrender. At the foot of the Cross he had a redemption take place within him whereby he became not only a good Christian, but a healthy, vital man.

You may look like the healthiest person in the world. But, you know, it is the mark of a sophisticated man not to reveal outwardly the inner frustrations of his life. And there may be people who are making themselves ill and are encouraging other maladies and diseases by unhealthy thinking. The solution is to affirm the life force; think the thoughts of God; cast out all hate; take in love.

The most curative thought in the world is the thought of love. Just go around loving people. Cast out all negative thoughts and fill the mind with positive thoughts. Cast out all inferiority thoughts. Fill the mind with victorious thoughts. Healthy mindedness is what makes people healthy, vital and alive.

One summer Sunday years ago I was preaching in a Presbyterian church in East Orange, New Jersey. After the service a woman came up to me and said, "I listened to your sermon, but I want to tell you that I itch all over."

"Madam, I've had many results from my sermons, but that's the most remarkable one I ever had."

She paid no attention to this but continued, "It's a strange thing. I itch a great deal, but I itch worse when I'm in church. I sometimes feel I should not come to church because I itch so badly."

"Maybe it's the cushions in the pews," I said.

"No," she replied, "I've taken it up with my doctor, and it's not that. I just itch all the time, and it shows as a kind of eczema on my skin." She bared her arm and said, "Take a look at that."

I looked at her arm. "There's not a thing there."

"Now, sir," she said, "don't tell me there isn't anything there. Can't you see it?"

"No. There's no eczema that I can see."

"Well," she insisted, "I itch all the time."

She interested me and I asked her to give me the name of her doctor. That turned out to be even more interesting. He said that this woman had a low-grade fever most of the time. It ran about 100°.

"What's wrong with her?" I asked. "She says she itches."

"Yes," the doctor said, "she's got eczema."

"But I didn't see any evidence of it on her arm."

"Oh," he replied, "it isn't on her arms. It's on her insides. It's in the mind. She has eczema of the thoughts."

"I never heard of that disease before," I said.

"You won't find it in any list of diseases, but that's what is wrong with her—eczema of the thoughts." I asked how he came upon it and he said, "This woman has a virulent, violent, evil hatred of her sister. She feels that her sister defrauded her when they probated their father's will. She hasn't spoken to her sister for twenty years. She is absolutely foul on the inside with her hate."

"What about the temperature, what causes that?" I asked.

"It is caused by the instability of her entire system," he said. "The body is trying to throw off this hate." Then he added, "As long as she has appealed to you, why don't you give her the catharsis-from-sin treatment?" This doctor used the most astonishing phrases.

So I asked the lady to come to my office. "Your doctor says you are filled with sin."

"I'll get another doctor," she retorted.

"Yes," I said, "you surely will. You've got one now." And I explained to her the mechanism of what was going on in her mind and how it affected her body. She listened; she struggled against it; but finally she saw and accepted it. One day I suggested she get down on her knees and surrender her hatred; and to do this she needed to pray lovingly about her sister. She resisted, she died hard. It was very difficult. You cannot let go of an unhealthy thought easily, because it wants to master you. But finally she turned and faced toward the Cross and the Blessed

Lord Jesus and said, "Jesus, forgive me, a sinner, and save me by Your grace. Cleanse me."

Gently I talked to her. "That isn't enough. Tell the Lord you love your sister." That was the hardest thing. But the day came when the two sisters walked down the aisle of my church arm in arm. And always they smile up at me in the pulpit. They have found forgiveness and a new love for one another. The doctor tells me this woman is completely well. You can't allow yourself the luxury of nursing evil thoughts and actions, because they will ultimately destroy you.

Isn't it interesting that the New Testament is so full of references about healing? Jesus Christ went around healing people, and, remember, He also went around exorcising devils from them. These weren't little men with tails and horns and forks. These devils were evil thoughts, evil ways, evil attitudes, that were making people sick. Jesus Christ is truly the Great Physician. He knows more about the intricacies of the human mind and body than any other physician who ever lived. He can heal you and keep you healed. He can heal me and keep me healed.

Try living one day without any unhealthy thoughts. You will have the time of your life. It may be very difficult, and the next day you may not want to try it over again because it will have made you tired; but try it another day, until it becomes habitual. Life will have a new dimension: it will bring you a healthy, happy and alive feeling. *But they that wait upon the Lord shall renew their strength; they shall mount up with wings as eagles; they shall run, and not be weary; and they shall walk, and not faint.*

God wants you to be healthy, vital and alive.

6. HOW TO COPE WITH MONEY WOES

Among the many letters which I receive each day I can always be sure that there will be a good percentage of them from people trying to cope with money problems. Though the number increases in hard times, balancing the budget always is a struggle for a good many people no matter what our economic situation. Answering these letters has always been difficult for me and I used to be tempted to reply by saying that I was a minister, concerned with spiritual matters, that financial difficulties lay outside my province. But then I realized that though I could give very little advice about solving the actual money problems, I could suggest a spiritual approach.

Not long ago, a letter came to me from a young housewife who said that she and her husband were talking about ending their two-year marriage. "All we seem to do any more is fight," she lamented.

Reading on I came to the heart of the matter. They had

got themselves so tangled in installment buying that their young romance had turned from bliss into one endless spindle of bills. It became apparent to me that these people didn't need a divorce court but rather a little straight thinking on the subject of finances. Here are some suggestions I gave them which might be helpful to anyone looking for a new approach in this area:

1. Remind yourself that you will never solve a money problem by remaining in a state of worry. You need to think creatively and it is impossible to develop creative thoughts out of a mind that is agitated. Therefore, ask God to give you a peaceful mind through which He can send an answer to your problem.

2. Remind yourself that God has the power to supply all your needs out of His vast abundance. If only a little trickle has been coming through to you from God's storehouse of prosperity, it may be that negative thoughts are preventing the supply ducts from being fully opened.

3. Ask yourself if you are thinking lack. There is a curious law that if you think lack you tend to create a condition of lack. Shift your thought pattern to one of abundance and believe that God is now in the process of giving you the abundance you need. Repel all lack thoughts, practice abundance thoughts. In ways that will amaze you, your needs will begin to be satisfied.

4. Seek to have complete family co-operation on expenses. Make yours a family budget to be family-spent. That is, Mary had a pair of shoes last month, so John gets a new shirt this month. Plan and pray over your expenditures as a family, and each member will feel pride and co-operation as the budget is controlled and spent on the basis of a new efficiency.

5. The word "thrift" may seem old-fashioned to some people, but I believe it is the most logical answer to most of our money problems. This, of course, may not be easy, but it is good for us to deny ourselves. Pray and ask God,

"Do I really need this?" The pleasure of giving up something now and saving for the future adds delight to life. Prayer control of spending brings both financial and spiritual blessings.

6. Try this specific action. Lay out all your bills before you on the table. Then ask God what to do about them. Ask Him for a definite plan of financing. Then make a plan of payment, economy, saving and spending on the basis of the insight you receive through your prayers.

7. Are you giving a tithe—one tenth—to God's work? That may seem a good deal, but a tithe sets in motion forces which will bring God's abundance toward you. Meditate upon God's promise: *Bring ye all the tithes into the storehouse . . . and prove me now herewith, saith the Lord of hosts, if I will not open you the windows of heaven, and pour you out a blessing, that there shall not be room enough to receive it.**

* *Malachi 3:10*

7. HOW TO COPE WITH DISCOURAGEMENT

If you are discouraged I have news for you—good news. You do not need to continue so, not at all. There is a way to end discouragement. And the word itself gives the clue.

"Discouragement" is formed by putting the prefix *dis* before the word *courage*, which means a discounting of courage. Therefore the way to end discouragement is to remove the prefix and to lay under your life a solid foundation of courage. Winston Churchill, that marvelous genius in the use of the English language, expresses it well. He says, "Success is never final. Failure is never fatal. It's courage that counts."

One reason why people suffer from discouragement is that they are subject to the natural ebb and flow of human emotion. There is a cyclic rise and fall in everything. This is the way man and nature are made. There is a cyclic rise and fall in the tides of the sea twice in every twenty-four hours. Pilots who fly in the upper levels of the atmosphere tell me that there is a clearly defined cycle in the ebb and flow of the great rivers of wind. There is a cyclic rise and fall in plant life with the seasons of the year. Everywhere in life is the cycle: the ebb and the rise and the flow.

The same is operative in human nature. There are times when the body is down and there are times when the body is up. This is manifestation of the cycle that is built into the construction of the human physique.

Cycles are also to be found in a person's mental and spiritual life. There is a normal range for this where the cycle goes below the median line and then goes above. But if an individual's mood goes too high and then too low, he is of the manic-depressive type. High exaltation may reach certain extremes where a person imagines he is Julius Ceasar or Abraham Lincoln—or he may go so low into the depths of depression that his mind tells him he is a worm, that he amounts to nothing. That dismal blackness is due to an abnormal flow of the cycle. But there is simple exaltation and a gray blackness which are fairly normal. People are victimized, motivated and conditioned by their moods.

But we are not supposed to be conditioned by our moods. We, the children of God, are supposed to control our moods, to take charge of them. You know, one of the greatest things about the Christian religion is what it can do with you if you really take it, if you really trust it, if you really live it. What a pity that the Christian religion is presented so widely today as a genial, nice philosophy, but with no power in it. There are so few who are reminding people of the tremendous power that Jesus Christ can let loose in a human being, power that can change even the cyclic rise and fall of your mental and emotional life so that you become a normal, controlled human being, not the victim of your moods, but the master of the same.

Through Him you can take your cycle, the rise and the

fall, and peg it at any point you wish. You may think this is too ideal, but it is for sure. You can peg it at a point where, despite anything that comes, you can have happiness and peace and power. You do not need to be the victim of discouragement at all if you get Jesus Christ in your heart and in your mind. So really take Him, really lock yourself up with Him. Really go for Him. Commit yourself to Him. This is the answer.

I remember a man who used to come often to Marble Collegiate Church. He sat about four or five pews from the front. A buyer from the Midwest, he bought for one of the largest chain stores in the country—and I often wondered how he could do the job successfully, because he was by all odds one of the most disturbed and gloomy men I ever met. You could tell he was partially sick, because this was not normal discouragement—this was an abnormal discouragement.

Every once in a while in preaching you find yourself eyeing one particular face. This man's countenance attracted my attention because of the utter disconsolateness written on it. It was both pathetic and in a sense repulsive. His face was tightened up in a knot, and it seemed as though a gray veil was hanging down over him. He would listen to me intently and this bothered me too, because his expression never changed, except maybe to grow more despondent. I was challenged and I really worked on him. Ordinarily you don't single out any person in a congregation, but in this instance I really did. I got nowhere.

Then one day he asked to see me and from then on we had a number of talks. This man was really disorganized on the inside. He was subject to wildly fluctuating moods. I urged him to read his Bible regularly and to pray. After a while I began to notice a gradual change, and within two or three years you would not have known him for the same man. He would sit in front of me on a Sunday morning

32

with his face fairly shining with joy. It was an amazing transformation.

One day I asked him what had happened. He said, "It was all through something you said one Sunday morning in your sermon." That sort of set me up, but he quickly added, "It wasn't anything you thought up. It was a quotation from the 23rd Psalm: 'He restoreth my soul . . .' "

The great thing about preaching is that you never know what a few simple words will do for somebody. Christ Himself said, "Heaven and earth shall pass away; but my words shall not pass away." And why? Because they are so powerful. Let a sentence out of the Bible explode in your consciousness and it can change your life. And that is what happened to this man.

When he started thinking about the words "He restoreth my soul" he said to himself, "I need to be restored. My soul . . . what is it? It is me. It is my psyche, it is my essence, it is my self, it is my personality." Every morning before he arose he would lie in bed and say out loud three times just this: "Thank You, for You have restored my soul. Thank You, for You have restored my soul. Thank You, for You have restored my soul." And this changed him from a man of discouragement to a man of such electric, magnetic faith that it permeated the more than one thousand employees of a great Midwestern store. He was no longer the victim of his moods.

What happened to him can happen to you, to me, to any of us. Have you ever honestly, forthrightly, committed your life to Jesus Christ? Perhaps you have been attending church for years and listening about Jesus. Perhaps you have read about Him. That is good. But have you ever given yourself to Him? That is what does it. If it didn't, this Gospel would never have lasted. These promises don't fail. He will restore your soul—if you give yourself to Him. That is the way to end discouragement. I guarantee it.

There is another thing: that nobody can live successfully without. It is a philosophy of life. You have to have a philosophy of life that takes cognizance of the fact that in this world there is trouble. I have lived for quite a while and I have never seen any time when there wasn't trouble. There is always trouble in this world. The Bible says that "man is born unto trouble, as the sparks fly upward." It also says, however, ". . . but be of good cheer; I have overcome the world." And we too have to overcome. You have to overcome your share of the trouble in this world.

But why is there so much trouble in the world? Suppose you had been God. Would you have put so much trouble in the world? Of course you wouldn't. If you were God right now, and if I were God, we'd take all the trouble out of the world, wouldn't we? That would be great, wouldn't it, if there was no trouble in the world and everything was "sweetness and light"? Wouldn't that be great? Well, the question is: would it? I am not forgetting that there are some people who suffer unduly. There is great injustice in the world and overwhelming hardship—and people victimized by these must have our support. But your philosophy must recognize the fact that your life is going to be made out of trouble.

Some years ago I wrote a book called *The Power of Positive Thinking* in which I tried to convey Biblical truths in modern, everyday language. Now the ministry is a profession in which you must never do anything differently from the way it has customarily been done unless you are prepared to suffer all sorts of calumnies until the time comes round. In all advances in theology somebody gets hurt. If you even say things in a different language in religion, some people don't like it. They want you to give them the old words. They make a whole religion of semantics. It isn't what you say; it is how you say it. Well, I felt that there were millions of people in America who didn't understand the theological language, so I tried to cast

34

great Christian principles in simple, workable form. And I was getting many brickbats from high echelons in the clergy and I was depressed and unhappy about it.

Then one day, when I was feeling particularly sorry for myself because somebody had leveled a new attack on me, I met a friend by the name of Herbert Clarke. This man was an adventurer who had been through several revolutions in Mexico and elsewhere, a man years my senior. He was an indomitable character. Meeting me on the street that day, he said, "What's the matter with you Norman? You look down in the mouth. You're not your usual self."

I told him some of the bitter criticism I was getting. I thought he would say, "Oh, that's too bad, my friend. Never mind. You've got lots of friends." But he didn't say that at all. You know what he said? He said, "Congratulations! Why, when you stir up that much opposition, that's when you know you're really doing something! There's nothing in the world like a good fight! Stand up for your convictions! You'll grow bigger doing it." And he hit me a clap on the back that nearly knocked me over and proceeded on his way.

Now that was a lot better for me than any amount of sweetness-and-light sympathizing. Herbert Clarke was a philosopher. He knew that the best way to end discouragement is to rise to the challenge your difficulties offer.

Get a philosophy of life. That is the thing that counts. Trouble is here. It is for a purpose. Use it for the purpose for which it was intended—to help you grow. Thank God for your troubles and remember the words "He restoreth my soul . . ." Feel God's restoration of your soul bringing you to a place where He gives you serenity, peace and powerful control. This is the way to end discouragement.

8. HOW TO COPE WITH GRIEF AND LONELINESS

Many people feel that when bereavement comes there is not much they can do about it, that it is something that just has to be endured, numbly and passively. This is not so. Nobody can minimize the fact of death. Of all the realities, it is the most real and poignant. But I don't think we are meant to sit and brood, or simply give in to grief. I think there are several things that can be done to lessen or minimize the shock. I want to list some of those things here, because in any program practical results require systematic application of basic principles, and a program to cope with sorrow is no exception. The first three recommendations have to do with your state of mind. The last five are practical, specific things that you can do to help cope with grief and loneliness.

1. Accept the fact that you are in a state of shock.

The loss of a loved one is often referred to as "a blow."

That is exactly what it is, an emotional blow that affects the spirit the same way that a crushing blow on the head affects the body. For a while you are going to be dazed. None of your reactions will be as in normal life. In a way, this numbness is a merciful thing, because it deadens the psychic pain while it lasts. But no one who has lost a loved one should expect to feel the same as always, or apologize for behavior that is temporarily erratic or different.

2. Despite your grief and sense of loss, try setting aside a few moments each day in which you open your mind to certain philosophical realizations.

There are certain inevitabilities in life, and death is one of them. It comes to all of us sooner or later; we all share it, and this universal sharing in itself is a comforting thing. Remind yourself that every life has many phases, from the cradle to the grave, each making its contribution to the sum of personality. Sorrow is one of these phases, and an important one, since it furnishes the contrasts whereby joy can shine so brightly. Remember, finally, that the way in which you receive your sorrow may affect, for good or bad, your entire subsequent life. You can emerge from it stronger and deeper and more mature, as your loved one would hope and want you to be, or you can remain confused and weakened and embittered. The choice is yours.

3. Hold the thought that adversity can be turned into spiritual power if it is met with faith and courage.

The famous American missionary, E. Stanley Jones, once told of a remarkable sight he witnessed in a remote, mountainous place in India. Late one afternoon he found himself in the path of an approaching storm. Winds of enormous strength were mounting, and all the small birds in the landscape took to cover. They crept under fallen logs. They burrowed into protective grasses. But then

37

Jones saw an eagle fly up into a tree. There it sat, facing the storm, arching its great wings slightly. When the winds howled down, those angled wings lifted the eagle effortlessly high into the heavens. While the lesser birds cowered and hid from sight, the eagle soared up into the clouds and rose above the storm.

So don't try to hide from your grief, or run from it. Face up to it with as much courage as you can muster, and the mighty power of faith will come to lift you above it as the storm lifted the eagle.

These attitudes and these desired states of mind will not come automatically to the bereaved person. There must be a conscious effort to attain them. In addition, there are certain definite, practical techniques that should be attempted.

4. Try prayer power.

The most important single step in facing sorrow is to ask Jesus Christ to assuage your anguish and believe that He does so. The greatest of all antidotes to grief is to believe that Christ can and will administer His healing balm to your wounded heart. This is accomplished through earnest and continual prayer. Under the harsh circumstances, it may be hard for you to pray. But just pour all your misery out to Him as a child who is hurt would cry out to an earthly parent.

5. Another technique that I strongly recommend is this: saturate yourself with the Scriptures.

They are full of comfort, strength and understanding.

A man came to see me who had just lost his son, and grief still effected him so that he could barely speak. "People tell me that it was the will of God," he said. "They say that I should be resigned. But these suggestions don't help. Can anything help?"

38

"Let me tell you," I said, "what helped a person with a problem of sorrow similar to yours." And I told him about a woman I knew who lost her daughter suddenly and tragically. The young woman was killed in a fall from a horse. She broke her neck, lingered only a few minutes and died. When the mother learned that her daughter was dead, she left the hospital and drove blindly away from the city. Late that night she came to a country inn and asked for a room. She paced the floor in her agony of spirit. On the bureau was a Gideon Bible. Something made her open it at random; she found herself staring at the beginning of the Book of Psalms.

She read the first Psalm, "And he shall be like a tree planted by the rivers of water . . ." She kept on reading, "The Lord is my shepherd; I shall not want. He maketh me to lie down in green pastures: he leadeth me beside the still waters." The heat went down in the old inn; the room grew cold. She took a blanket from the bed, wrapping it around her against the chill. She read on in fascination and with a strange sense of peace. "So teach us to number our days, that we may apply our hearts unto wisdom . . . For he shall give his angels charge over thee." She read all the way through these magnificent poems of faith and hope and courage to the very last verse, "Let every thing that hath breath praise the Lord. Praise ye the Lord."

Later she said to me, quite simply, "That reading of the Psalms did something very wonderful to me. All of life was there, joy and sorrow, happiness and heartbreak. I found my answers deep and satisfying. My heart was comforted. When I started reading, I wanted to die; when I finished, I wanted to live."

That's what the Scriptures can do for someone who is sorrowing. But I think it has to be a massive dose. A verse or two or a chapter or two isn't enough. It's like those antibiotics that doctors prescribe, doubling the quantity in the first dose so that the healing agent can get into the bloodstream quickly and fight the infection. That's what the Bible is: spiritual medicine. And the reason people have turned to it over the centuries is the reason why any good medicine is prescribed and sought after. It works. It heals wounded minds and hearts.

6. Give expression to your grief.

Plainly speaking, cry about it. We Anglo-Saxons are too quick to equate a display of emotion with weakness. Actually, the old phrase "to vent one's emotions" is a good one, for this method of relief is nature's safety valve. If you repress grief too sternly, serious emotional maladjustment may result.

I'm not advocating ostentatious public displays of grief; some degree of control is called for. But in privacy, or with family or close friends, it is often better to let grief flow out in visible form before it can congeal within. As a wise man once said, a tear is agony in solution. And there are times when it can also be, temporarily at least, a solution to your agony. Jesus Himself wept when He heard that His friend Lazarus was dead. We should not be ashamed to do likewise.

7. Go on living normally.

Some people find this very hard to do. They even seem to feel that it involves some disrespect or lack of affection for the loved one who has died. But I'm convinced that this is shallow thinking—a mistaken point of view. Surely the person who has died would want his loved ones on earth to carry on the torch of life; he would not want to feel that he was the cause of any curtailment or diminution of living.

In any case, normalcy, the carrying out of familiar and necessary tasks, is in itself a steadying and comforting thing. During World War II a young Royal Air Force flier was killed in action. In one of his last letters to his father he wrote: "You have your work to carry on, and if anything happens to me you must go on without losing a day. Do you understand? That'll keep you straight on the track, and if you keep steady it'll help Mummy more than anything else you can do for her." Prophetic words—and profoundly true, as the sorrowing father later learned.

Some people shrink from going to places that remind them of their loved one; others shrink from doing things that they once did together, especially as husband and wife. This is understandable, because it does sharpen the sense of physical loss. The antidote is to remind yourself that the loved person is not only still with you, in a spiritual sense, but is far more constantly with you than was possible when he was alive. When my wife Ruth called me on the telephone to tell me that my mother had died, she said, "I know you'll find this hard to believe right now, Norman, but your mother is going to be with you and nearer to you from now on to a far greater degree than she ever was before. In the past, you have always made plane trips or train trips to be with her for a few days or even a few hours. Now she can be with you always." This was true, and once I was able to grasp it my sense of grief and loss was vastly diminished.

Now and then you find someone who has an almost morbid tendency to cling to the past. One day, before a Rotary Club meeting in a New York hotel, I saw the widow of a friend and fellow-Rotarian sitting forlornly in the lobby. I asked her what she was doing there. "Oh," she said sadly, "I come and sit here every week on Rotary day, because I know that this is where Fred used to be."

"Well," I said, "wait for me until after the meeting, because I have something to say to you."

When the luncheon was over, I took her by the arm and led her to a taxi. "Where are we going?" she asked.

"We're going down to my church," I told her. "There

41

are some overworked women down there addressing en-velopes. They need help, and you're going to give it to them. Fred would much rather have you do something like that than sit in a hotel lobby feeling sorry for yourself! Maybe you'd better start acting the way Fred would want you to do." She came along quite meekly, and later told me that the sense of companionship and usefulness that she got eased her grief more than anything else.

Of course it did! The human mind can only hold one thought at a time. So if you are busy and useful, if your attention is focused outside of yourself, there is less room in your mind for inward-focused grief. That's where the pain is: in your mind. It's not disloyal to try to diminish that pain. Your loved one would be the first to urge you to do so.

8. The best of all ways to get your mind off your own troubles is to try to help someone else with his.

As the old Chinese proverb says, "When I dig another out of trouble, the hole from which I lift him is the place where I bury my own."

I knew a woman once whose dearly loved husband died. They were childless and very close to each other. The worst time of day, she told me, was supper-time, when she had taken great pleasure in fixing food that he liked. She was a fine cook, but she found she had little interest in cooking for herself alone. Then one evening she said to herself, "This is no good. I'm going into that kitchen and bake a cake just the way Harry liked it. Then I'm going to take that cake, and decorate it with candles, and take it down to the children's ward at the hospital. And tomorrow night I'm going to bake some pies and take them to the orphanage, and the night after that I'll make cookies and take them to some friend who has lost a loved one, and I'm going to keep that up until I feel like myself again!"

42

That story had a remarkable ending. One of the recipients of the widow's cakes was a banker who was highly impressed, not only with the woman's selflessness, but with the quality of her baking. "Why don't you go into this commercially?" he asked her.

"Because I don't have any capital or any experience," she replied.

"I can arrange the capital," he said, "and I don't think you need any experience." The result was a small but profitable business venture and an adjusted, outgoing, useful life.

Carrie Chapman Catt used to have a prescription for curing the blues. It went something like this: "Go to your room; put on your hat; go out and do something for someone. Repeat ten times."

You don't have to limit that prescription to any one area of living. It works in all of them.

9. HOW TO COPE WITH DEFEAT

Do you feel defeated by anything? The answer to that question must, of necessity, be that sometimes we do. Well, you don't need to be defeated by anything—and I weigh those words carefully and objectively.

The only time you need to be concerned about defeat is when you accept defeat. If you are willing to settle for a defeated situation, then all the factors of defeat will be involved in that situation. There is a power in this world called the power of defeat, or the power of frustration, or the power of disappointment. Everybody knows this. But there is an even greater power in this world beside which these powers fall into insignificance. And this power nobody ought ever to forget. It is the enormous power of God and the illimitable power of faith in the Lord Jesus Christ. By this power you can circumvent and overcome any defeat you will ever have to face.

This isn't to minimize circumstances. Life is very tough. It can be almost overwhelming. Shakespeare wrote, "When sorrows come, they come not single spies, but in battalions." There are times when life seems to throw the whole book at you. And if you are in one of those situations now it may seem incredible that anyone would say, "Never accept defeat." But if you don't want to be defeated you don't accept it. It's just that simple.

I am reminded of a man whom I happened to encounter one evening on the steps of the Masonic Temple on Nob Hill in San Francisco. This encounter was a very inspirational one for me. I had just finished talking to about 2,000 salesmen in that beautiful auditorium. There was another speaker following me, but I could not remain for that part and had to leave the meeting. On the steps outside this man approached me. "I came here tonight to hear you," he said, "because I believe in your philosophy that you never need to be defeated. And I just wanted to tell you that you are so right!"

He proceeded to enlighten me on his own personal experience. He was a little racy in the way he talked, but he was deeply spiritual. "I took an awful beating and retreated to lick my wounds," he said. "Life just ganged up on me and I felt I was completely through. I wandered for days in a deep gloom.

"But finally I decided I couldn't live that way. So my wife and I started a little program. We decided that every morning we would read the Bible for fifteen minutes. We started with Matthew and read the New Testament all the way through. After each reading we had a quiet time and we prayed and put ourselves in God's hands.

"I wish you would tell people whenever you get the chance that if they will only do this, nothing can ever defeat them. Out of this period of prayer and meditation and Bible reading I got some ideas. And these ideas helped me rebuild."

He was a very rapid speaker and threw these things off very fast. I didn't want to interrupt the flow of his thought, but immediately after this conversation I went to the hotel and wrote down the points he gave me. And I tell you this formula is worth practicing. Here is what happened to this man.

"First," he said, "there came a day when I made a decision. I decided that I would never accept defeat." (And the minute he did that he was on the way.)

"Then I decided to start thinking creatively and spiritually and not emotionalize negatively." (It is a step forward when you start thinking and stop emotionalizing about a defeat.)

"Next I stopped feeling sorry for myself, because I had to admit that I had actually come to the point where I was enjoying self pity." (And so many people make this mistake.)

"Then I decided to stop asking *why* and *if* and to start asking *how*." (This is very significant, because when anything happens to you that is difficult there is a tendency to think, "Why did this have to happen to me?" or "If only this hadn't happened!" Forget that. Skip it! Pass it by and start thinking from then on, "*How* will I meet the situation that exists?")

"Next I got reacquainted with the God of the new start." (That is terrific: the God of the new start.)

"Then I got God's directions on how to rebuild."

"Finally," he added vigorously, "I got going."

Before we parted he said, "I want to witness to you that I am a Christian. Oh, I've got my imperfections, but I am all out for Jesus Christ, because He is all out for me, and I really go for Him because of what He will do for any human being." There was a full moon over San Francisco that night and the little bells of the cable cars were clanking as they came up the hill. It was fresh and clear and everything was bright and beautiful—but more beautiful than anything else was the look on the face of this man who had decided never to accept defeat.

46

"And I've got a text for you," he concluded. I was interested to see what this text would be, and I wasn't surprised when I got it, because this is a tremendous text. It is in Philippians—4th chapter, 13th verse—and the King James Version has it this way: "I . . ." You have to draw yourself up tall to say this text; you can't do it sitting down. "I . . ." (Me, myself) "I can do . . ." (Now hold on tight!) "all things. . . ." It doesn't say a few things; it doesn't say some things. The Christian religion as taught by Jesus has a great deal more power in it than most of its followers ever use. "I can do all things . . ." not by your own strength, but "through Christ which strengtheneth me."

The version of the Bible put out by the American Bible Society, called *Good News for Modern Man*, says it differently but just as dynamically, "I have the strength to face all conditions by the power that Christ gives me." That describes who you are and what you are offered. Talk about being defeated! It is really unworthy of a Christian to say, "Well, I guess I've had it. It's too much for me. I can't handle it anymore. I will just accept defeat."

"Oh," you say, "but look at all the difficulties." I am looking at them. You ask, "Does this apply socially?" Of course it applies socially. Our forefathers made a new world. Were our forefathers any greater than we are? We too can make a new world if we think we can and if we have the same quality of faith as they had. No, we don't need to be defeated by anything. Never accept defeat.

So how do you go about working this out in a practical manner? The whole thing is practical, but we are going to be even more practical. You use three principles. The first is the *never-think-defeat* principle. The second is the *stick-it-out-and-never-stop-trying* principle. And the third is the *keep-God-in-it* principle. It is of course an established fact that we are what we think. I have no crystal ball, nor do I read tea leaves or palms, but do you

47

know something? I can tell you precisely and exactly what you will be ten years from now. That is easy; that is simple. What you think in the next ten years will determine what you are. What you are today is what you have been thinking for the last ten, twenty, thirty, forty, fifty years.

If you feel defeated and you think, "I'm tired and weary and I've had it," that is exactly how it will be. You can count on it for sure. You will be what you accept in your mind. But if, on the contrary, when the going gets hard and difficult, you think, "I won't accept this—I will continue to think victory and not defeat," then what happens is that all the resources of your nature flow toward effecting a victory situation and circumventing a defeat condition.

We had a man in Marble Collegiate Church once who was a dreamer—a businessman, but a dreamer. He had a great dream. Frankly, his dream seemed to me bigger than he was, and he was defeated time after time. I never knew a man to have so many setbacks. But did he ever stop dreaming his dream? Not at all! I asked him one day how he managed to have this attitude. "Oh, it's very simple," he answered "every day of my life I pass a series of faith thoughts through my mind and this keeps me hoping, believing and struggling."

So the first principle is the never-think-defeat principle. One way to cancel out defeat thoughts is simply to repeat that text from Philippians 4:13. It will knock any defeatism out of you. "I can do all things through Christ which strengtheneth me."

The second principle is the stick-it-out-and-never-stop-trying principle. This is almost like primary-school talking, but how many times have you failed at something because you simply didn't try hard enough or long enough? The test of an individual's character is how tenacious he is. The attitude to take is the attitude of a bull

48

dog: you get hold of an idea and never let go. If you have a dream, if you have an objective, and road blocks are in the way, you have to have a strategy. When you are blocked you must get around or underneath, or over, or through the thing. No road block should stop you. You must keep on going. Many a time I have seen that tragedy of human life where somebody would have achieved a great thing if he had just kept at it a little bit longer. Success was just out there at the end of his outstretched fingers but he couldn't quite feel it because he was so tired and discouraged that he let go. If he had lunged for it, if he had tried once more, he would have had it! It is the stick-to-it, keep-at-it, never-give-up principle.

One summer vacation Mrs. Peale and I were in England and went down to Chartwell, the old home of Winston Churchill, which is now open to the public. We had a very special guide, a woman who had been in Churchill's household, as the British say, ever since she was a little girl. She was the daughter of the chief overseer of the estate. She had known Churchill intimately, like a father, and you could see that she was devoted to his memory. As she showed us around the house, she would touch very lovingly things that the great man had used. Presently she said, "Come out on the lawn with me. I want you to stand in a certain place." She took us to a spot where one could look out over the wealds of Kent and see the low hills in the distance. "This is where he used to come and stand each night during the war and watch the Nazi bombers come over at twilight. He would stand here with a big cigar in his mouth and a cane in his hand, his stocky legs spread apart, as he watched the planes pass overhead. A moment later you could hear the reverberation of bombs falling on London and see flames shooting up against the night sky. His face was always grim."

"Do you think there was ever a time when Sir Winston contemplated the possibility of defeat?" I asked her.

49

She was a very reserved, austere kind of woman, but at this she actually laughed out loud. "Sir Winston thinking defeat? That is impossible! Sir Winston never entertained the idea of defeat. He would always say, 'Tomorrow will be better. The day will come when we will win. The final victory will be ours!' " Amen

"Where did you say he stood?" I asked. She showed me and I got my feet firmly fixed in his footsteps, because that kind of indomitability appeals to me.

Afterwards I thought about the time Churchill was invited to speak to the boys at Harrow, his old school. The headmaster had told the boys that Churchill was coming and that he would give an immortal message. "Bring your notebooks," he told the boys, "and copy down everything he says. You will want to pass it along to your children and your grandchildren because you are going to hear the greatest living Englishman."

Well, the day came and Churchill arrived. He was well along in years now. He stood on the platform and put his fingers in his vest-pockets as was his custom, then pulled his glasses down on his nose as he often did, and looked them all over. As he stood there looking at the rough, wooden benches in which initials had been carved for six-hundred years, his own carved among them, he no doubt saw in memory a little boy who had sat there many years before, a shy, skinny little kid named Winston Churchill, who stuttered—but who became subsequently the greatest master of English speech in modern history.

He noticed how bright they looked, but realized that life could bring them plenty of hard knocks and troubles. So he made his speech. "Never give in, never give in, never, never, never, never!" And he sat down. An immortal speech had been made which they would remember to the end of their days.

Never give in! You don't need to, for the Lord God will

help you. And you can overcome all conditions through the power given you by Christ. So that is the second principle, the stick-it-out-and-never-give-up principle.

Finally, the third principle is the keep-God-in-it principle. Nobody can be as strong, vital and heroic as I have suggested without the presence of God. This is a big, overwhelming world and we are very small. It is like the prayer the Normandy fishermen offer when they go out on the deep to fish. Before they cast off their little boats they pray, "O Lord, take care of us. The sea is so vast. We are so small." And He does and He will. I tell you, friends, from the bottom of my heart: the secret of meeting life victoriously is how close you are to God, how deeply and sincerely you receive Jesus Christ into your life. And I guarantee to you that if you give your life to God, if you commit your life to Christ, until this becomes your consuming passion, you will have an immunity—not from difficulty, but from defeat. And that is all we can ask.

That is what the Bible means where it says, "I can do all things through Christ which strengtheneth me," or "I have the strength to face all conditions by the power that Christ gives me." This is your faith, friends; this is your religion. Take it and live with it and never accept any defeat, because on the other side of defeat, if you don't accept it, there is a glorious victory.

10. HOW TO COPE WITH WORRY

Mrs. Peale and I were descending in an elevator one morning from the twenty-sixth floor of a hotel. At the twenty-fourth floor a young woman got on. The three of us were the only people in the elevator. I gathered from her dress that she was on the staff of the hotel. She was a charming, outgoing girl who wished us a "good morning."

We naturally answered in kind. She had such a genuine smile on her face that I said, "You seem to be a very happy person."

"Oh," she said, "yes, I guess so, but I don't know . . . I've got an awful lot of worrying to do today."

"Do you worry every day," I asked, "or is it just today?"

"No," she reflected, "it's a habit of mine. I worry every day." At that moment we came to the fifteenth floor and she got off and disappeared down the hall. Mrs. Peale asked if we shouldn't go back and look for her, but I thought that was pushing it a little far. So, I never was able to tell her what was on my mind, but I can tell you, and maybe through the providence of God some will be helped. But I have often thought, happy as she was and nice as she was, why in the world did she have the worry habit?

When you come right down to it, it's a very widespread malady. Some psychiatrist has declared that this is a generation of anxiety. And I understand there is a modern symphony called "The Age of Anxiety." Can you imagine that? Putting worry and fear to music!

One scientist declared that there are so many things today to be worried about, to be fearful of, that one of the pollutions of our time is a kind of free-floating anxiety that affects almost everybody. Some say it is because of the atom bomb or space missiles or air pollutants.

Let us set against this worry and anxiety tendency a marvelous statement from Isaiah 41:10, which says, "Fear thou not; for I am with thee." Reduced into common, everyday speech, it means, "Don't you be afraid, for you are not alone; I, your God, your Lord, am always with you."

Well, what steps can you take to stop the worry habit? This habit is nothing more nor less than an accumulation of worry thoughts. When a person has worried so often and so long about so many things, it becomes an habitual response or reaction. He is governed and motivated and dominated by worry. On the contrary, faith is the accumulation of faith thoughts, and the only thing in this world that is more powerful than fear is faith. So, in overcoming worry the secret is to begin the accumulation of faith thoughts: faith about everything, faith at all times, faith under all circumstances.

Whenever a fear or worry thought comes to mind, immediately cancel it out with a faith thought. This will retrain your mind so that in due course the worry habit will disintegrate and give way. You can break *any* habit.

And the best way to break a habit is to establish a corollary habit that is stronger. Anyone can do it if he *wills* to do it and will work at it and will ask the help of God.

Let me illustrate this. Some years ago Judge Harold Medina, a famous jurist in New York City, was assigned to preside over the trial of eleven U.S. communists who had been charged with conspiracy to overthrow the government of the United States. This trial was one of the first attempts of the communists to discredit and subvert the judiciary. The witnesses in the trial were insolent; the defense attorneys were devious; constant confusion reigned in the courtroom—until finally the judge became aware of the fact that they were more interested in breaking up the trial than in getting an acquittal. They wanted a mistrial and, beyond that, they wanted to destroy the judge himself, putting him under such a strain that he would break. All of the confusion, the hatred, the insolence was aimed at him.

In their attempt to destroy him, they began to research the life of Judge Medina, leaving no stone unturned from his boyhood on. They discovered, in their fiendish manner, that he was a victim of acrophobia, which means the fear of high places.

When he was a small boy, Harold Medina's father took him to Niagara Falls to see the great natural wonder. At the brink of the great abyss, Harold shrank back in terror. He could not go near that railing, for he was afraid he would fall over. The investigators found this out; they marshalled the mobs in Foley Square in front of the federal courthouse. When Medina stood at the window and looked down from the twenty-second floor of the building, he became aware of the mob shouting, "Medina will *fall*, like Forrestal." Only a short time before, Defense Secretary Forrestal had fallen to his death from a hospital window.

The word "fall" was used all around him; they underscored the word "fall" in letters and newspaper clippings; they hounded him with the word "fall," playing on his old fear. Finally came a night in his apartment when Mrs. Medina opened the window—it was a stifling night—and in terror he said, "Close that window, please, Ethel." And then he confessed to her the longtime fear he had of falling from high places. He kept the window open only a crack and remained awake all night, afraid he might fall as the mob was shouting at him to do.

But Medina was a Christian. He began to pray, and in his prayers he got the idea that the way to cancel out this fear was by faith, so he began to fill his mind with every conceivable faith thought. He saturated his consciousness with thoughts of faith; he affirmed God's protection and love. He was hounded through eleven months of the trial, but in the tenth month he found peace. Prayer alone kept him going. He lost his old fear, and presided in a way that brought great distinction to American jurisprudence.

Undoubtedly very few have had or will have such a dramatic experience as Judge Medina. But if this great man could discipline himself and put faith thoughts into his mind, thus eliminating fear thoughts, so can you; so can I. "Fear thou not; for I am with thee." In other words, "Don't be afraid, I'm by your side." That is the answer.

The second way to handle fear and worry is just not to take them supinely. You attack them. Do not let them push you around, overwhelming you all the time. *You* attack *them*. The best form of defense is to attack. So, if you have some fears, set them out in front of you, take a good look at them and say, "I'm attacking you in the name of the Lord Jesus. I'm finished with you. You don't dominate me any more." That is the way to talk.

I read at one time the life of General George Patton. It is a very interesting story. He was quite a man, one of the greatest military men this country has ever produced. And he was always running counter to the High Command, especially when they would tell him to retreat. He did not believe in retreat. He believed if an enemy was attacking in force, even with superior force, the best way to confuse and frustrate that enemy was to attack him hard, throw everything you had at him. That is what Patton proceeded to do in the Battle of the Bulge.

Well, I do not know anything about the military side of things, but I do know you can tangle your worries all up and confuse them by attacking with force and with a will to overcome. As a young boy, I suffered acutely from shyness. The thought of getting on a platform frightened me to death. If I got up before a half dozen people, my mouth would get dry, my knees would shake, my hands would tremble. It was terrible. So I tried to get over my shyness. All kinds of public speakers fascinated me, and I listened and observed them carefully. I even used to hear Teddy Roosevelt, which shows the date when we were operating!

Teddy Roosevelt was one of the most tremendous figures ever to appear in the United States. There was never anybody like him! He used to bite his words off incisively, compellingly.

But another speaker, while lacking Roosevelt's greatness, in my opinion, had a voice and manner that really drew me. William Jennings Bryan did not bite the words off; he rounded them; they were like liquid music in their beauty! And he could sing a word over the heads of 40,000 people without any such contraption as a microphone. Tremendous! I used to follow these men around whenever they were in our area, and one day I told my mother, "I want to be a public speaker."

My mother said, "Norman, if you want to be a public speaker you've got to attack your fears, and the only way to attack them is to 'do the thing you fear, and the death of fear is certain,' as Emerson said."

So I got up and made my poor little speeches. It was

terribly difficult at first, but I overcame the fear of doing it—or did I? For even today when I walk on a platform, there is my old enemy—the fear that I can't do it. Every once in a while my mouth gets dry. But now my faith is stronger than my fear. Maybe it is an everlasting fight from the cradle to the grave, but set those fears out in front of you and attack, and attack, and attack; and you will become master of them. Even if they gang up on you, attack them and victory will be yours.

Finally, the greatest of all surety factors against anxiety, worry and fear is to build up in your consciousness the fact that God is with you. This is the greatest, strongest thought a human being can get: "I, in this world in the midst of all this confusion, am not alone; therefore I'll not be afraid, for He is with me." That is what Christianity is all about, when you come right down to it. God is with you.

You and I have far more than a human friend. Human friends help. In time of trouble and difficulty it helps to see the beloved face of your wife, or your husband, or some dear friend who is with you in a time of need. But human support is weak; human support decays. The support of God is everlasting.

In Belgium I visited a Nazi prison camp called "The Breendonk." It is about half-way between Brussels and Antwerp, and it was the prison to which the Nazis took loyal Belgian citizens during World War II, where many died and all suffered great hardship and torture. My guide that day told me that one morning they came before daybreak and took his father to the Breendonk. He never saw him again. He showed me the wall in front of which he thinks his father was shot.

"How did these people imprisoned here endure the anxiety and fear and worry and injustice of this place?" I asked.

"They had a secret," he said.

"What was the secret?" I wanted to know.

He took me to a little cell, far back in a corner, where there was just a little slit in the stone wall. There were some high benches and he asked me to crawl with him under the benches. Then he took my hand and guided it to the stone wall. "Run your hand over what you feel here," he said.

"I feel a carving in the stone," I said.

"What you are feeling is the face of our Savior, Jesus Christ. These men and women, including my father, in the darkest hour of their hopelessness, would come here and put their hands on His Holy and Loving Face. And it was that which sustained them and gave them victory over their fears. It was their way of remembering that they were not alone." *body*

This is one of the most powerful, spiritual, psychological principles in the world. Get with Jesus! He is with you! And attack your fears; they cannot stand in His presence. "Fear thou not; for I am with thee . . ." That is the way to deal with worry and defeat it.